Make Me Laugh!

BACKYARD BEASTIES

JOKES TO SNAKE YOU SMILE

by Diane L. Burns and Peter and Connie Roop
pictures by Brian Gable

ℰ Carolrhoda Books, Inc. • Minneapolis

Q: Where do cats go for fun?

A: The a-mew-sment park.

Q: Where did the cat get his new toaster?

A: From a cat-alog.

Q: What did the cat pour on his hamburger?

A: Cat-sup.

Q: What do birds get after flight school?

A: Their wings.

Q: What kind of weather do mice hate?

A: When it rains cats and dogs.

Q: What do you call a bug dance?

A: A mothball.

Q: What is the richest snake in the world?

A: A diamondback.

Q: What snake can be mowed?

A: A grass snake.

Q: What do professional athlete reptiles wear on their feet?

A: Snakers.

Q: What kind of ants have trunks?

A: Eleph-ants.

Q: Which bug can you find in the alphabet?

A: B.

Q: What bird always forgets the words to a song?

A: A hummingbird.

Q: Why are rabbits always smiling?

A: Because they're hoppy.

Q: What kind of bugs can you find in a clock?

A: Ticks.

Q: What language do ticks speak?

A: Tick talk.

Q: What goes "hop, hop, hop, tumble, tumble, tumble"?

A: A clumsy frog trying to hop down stairs.

Q: What kind of bug has no wings but flies?

A: A spider.

Q: Which bug is related to you?

A: Your ant.

Q: What do young insects ride in?

A: Baby buggies.

Q: Where does a snake go to get a new skin?

A: To a shed.

Q: How do birds clean their beaks?

A: With toothpecks.

Q: Why did the bird go to Hollywood?

A: Because he wanted to be a starling.

Q: How do frogs play Ping-Pong?

A: With a lily paddle.

Q: What do frogs play on quiet afternoons?

A: Croakquet.

Q: What is a rabbit's favorite dance?

A: The bunny hop.

Q: What is a poisonous snake most afraid of?

A: Biting her tongue.

Q: What is the reptiles' professional basketball team?

A: Los Angeles Snakers.

Q: What do squirrels do in their free time?

A: Nuttin' much.

Q: What did the cat say when he fell on his face?

A: Me-OW!

Q: What did the mother grasshopper say to her children?

A: "Hop to it!"

Q: Do snakes need silverware when they eat?

A: No, they have forked tongues.

Q: What game do toads play with a rope?

A: Tug-of-wart.

Q: Where do frogs put their coats when they go to the theater?

A: In the croakroom.

Q: What track-and-field event do frogs excel at?

A: The tadpole vault.

Q: What kind of cat sucks on lemons?

A: A sourpuss.

Q: How does a bee brush its hair?

A: With its honeycomb.

Q: How did the rabbit feel when her brother stepped on her ear?

A: She was hoppin' mad.

Q: What is a squirrel's favorite ballet?

A: *The Nutcracker.*

Q: What kind of insects can dance?

A: Jitter-bugs.

Q: How do girl cats attract boy cats?

A: Purr-fume.

Q: Why did the frog kiss the photographer?

A: Because he wanted to become the handsome prints.

Q: What kind of bugs do knights fight?

A: Dragonflies.

Q: Why didn't any birds go to the duck doctor?

A: Because they said she was a quack.

Q: What does a snake conductor say at the train station?

A: "All a boa'd!"

Q: What happened to the squirrel that went crazy?

A: He lost his sa-nut-y.

Q: Why didn't the wren get an apartment?

A: Because the one he wanted was already wren-ted.

Q: What kind of cat lives underwater?

A: A catfish.

Q: What kind of guest towels will you find at a snake motel?

A: Hiss and Hers.

Q: What should you do if your frog breaks down?

A: Call a toad truck.

Q: What did the boy say to the mosquito?

A: "Don't bug me!"

Q: What do you get when you stack frogs on top of each other?

A: A toadem pole.

Q: What two cats live in the meadow?

A: Cat-tails and pussy-willows.

Q: How did the ugly toad reach the princess so he could kiss her?

A: He pulled up a toadstool.

Q: What kind of birds sit down?

A: Stool pigeons.

Q: What happened to the tourist snakes that got lost in Disneyland?

A: They got rattled.

Q: What kind of insect sleeps the most?

A: A bedbug.

Q: What kind of bugs are the sweetest?

A: Honeybees.

Q: Why was the bird arrested?

A: Because he was always robin somebody.

Q: How fast can a frog stick out his tongue?

A: In the wink of a fly.

Q: What kind of insects are the best singers?

A: Hum-bugs.

Q: What do ducks get in the mail?

A: Duckbills.

Q: What is the name of a famous bug rock group?

A: The Beetles.

Q: Why do birds save money?

A: So they can have a nice nest egg when they retire.

Q: What do you call a bird that drinks water?

A: A swallow.

Q: Did the kitten win the argument with his mother?

A: No. He was licked from the start.

Q: What do you call it when a kitten gets her tail caught in the door?

A: A cat-astrophe.

Q: What kind of bugs are the messiest?

A: Litterbugs.

Kitty: Can Tomcat come out and play?

Mother Cat: No, Tom's playing with a ball of string, and he'll be tied up all afternoon.

Smart Frog: What does a thief want to do to a bank?

Smarter Frog: Robbit.

Smart Frog: What should you do if you find a magic lamp?

Smarter Frog: Rubbit.

Q: What kind of music do the Beetles play?

A: Bee-bop.

Q: Where do birds relax in their houses?

A: On the front perch.

Q: What is a snake student's best subject in school?

A: Hisss-tory.

Diner: What is this spider doing in my soup?

Waiter: The backstroke!

Q: What do you get when you cross a bull with a frog?

A: A horned toad.

Q: What do get when you cross a frog with a pig?

A: A warthog.

Q: What's kitty's favorite subject in school?

A: Mew-sic.

Q: What kind of music do cats like?

A: Cat-chy tunes.

Q: Which sport do mosquitos like the best?

A: Skin diving.

Q: What has eighteen legs and catches flies?

A: A baseball team.

Q: Why do bugs hate baseball bats?

A: Because they're flyswatters.

Q: How does a squirrel store her nuts?

A: Bury carefully.

Q: How do you start a firefly race?

A: Ready, set, GLOW!

Q: Which of the fifty states has the largest population of snakes?

A: Hississippi.

Q: Where should you go if your frog needs glasses?

A: The hoptometrist.

Q: What should you do if a frog tells silly stories in his sleep?

A: Nothing. Let sleeping frogs lie.

Q: What does a cotton farmer call a bad beetle?

A: An evil weevil.

Q: What is worse than finding a worm in your apple?

A: Finding half a worm in your apple.

Q: What do you call an eight-armed cat?

A: An octo-puss.

Q: What do Robert the Cat's friends call him?

A: Bobcat.

Q: What kind of insects are always polite?

A: Ladybugs.

Q: What do you call a cat who dresses just like her friends?

A: A copycat.

Q: What did the boy centipede say to the girl centipede?

A: "I want to hold your hand, hand, hand, hand, hand . . . "

Q: What is a snake doing when it daydreams?

A: Hiss-ful thinking.

Q: Why don't sad rabbits jump?

A: Because they're unhoppy.

Q: What kind of cat has the most legs?

A: A cat-erpillar.

Q: What is a squirrel's favorite pastry?

A: Do-nuts.

Q: Why did the boy cat like the girl cat?

A: She was purr-fectly a-mew-sing.

Q: Why did the bird start boxing lessons?

A: Because he wanted to be a feather weight.

Q: What part of a snake has the most minerals?

A: Their copperheads.

Q: What has four wheels and flies?

A: A garbage truck.

Q: Do snakes make good race car drivers?

A: No, they are always making pit stops.

Q: What kind of animals hang out at the airport?

A: Flying squirrels.

Q: Why did the boy throw the butter out the window?

A: He wanted to see a butterfly.

Q: Why did the bird join the Boy Scouts?

A: Because he wanted to be an eagle scout.

Q: What's the nicest thing you can say to a frog?

A: Go jump in a lake.

Q: What kind of insects are good in school?

A: Spelling bees.

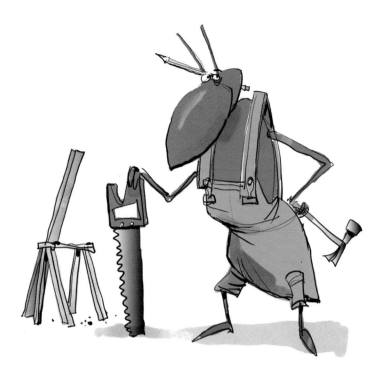

Q: What kind of insects are the best builders?

A: Carpenter ants.

Q: Why did the nine birds fly to Baltimore?

A: Because they wanted to become Orioles.

Q: What sport does a cat play with mice?

A: Squash.

Q: What kind of ants are the biggest?

A: Gi-ants.

Q: What kind of birds like to play in the outfield?

A: Flycatchers.

Q: Which insect has a hard time making up its mind?

A: A may-bee.

Q: Why do frogs always look nervous?

A: Because they have butterflies in their stomachs.

Q: What do cats like to do on hot summer afternoons?

A: Catnap.

Q: What do you call a cat that hangs out at the bowling lanes?

A: An alley cat.

Q: What do you get when you cross a frog with a calendar?

A: A leap year.

Q: What's a cat's favorite position on a baseball team?

A: Cat-cher.

Q: Where can you buy bugs?

A: At a flea market.

Emily: What has eighteen feet, red eyes, and long claws?

Anna: I don't know, what?

Emily: I don't know either, but it's crawling up your neck!

Q: How does a snake say "thank you"?

A: "Fangs a lot."

Q: What do frogs like to drink in the winter?

A: Hot croakoa.

Q: Where did the kittens go on their field trip?

A: The mew-seum.

Q: What did the cat teacher say to his silent student?

A: Cat got your tongue?

Q: What is a snake's favorite holiday?

A: Hiss-mas.

Q: What is a cat's favorite color?
A: Purr-ple.

Q: Why did the bird land on a plate?
A: Because she had a fork tail.

Q: What bird is a little flaky?
A: A snowy owl.

Q: What worm can never go into space?
A: An earthworm.

Q: What game do rabbits play?

A: Hopscotch.

Q: Why can't you weigh a firefly?

A: Because it's so light.

Q: Who should you call if you need to get in touch with a rabbit?

A: The hoperator.

Q: What do frogs hang above their doors on Christmas?

A: Mistletoad.

Q: What kind of insect uses a camera?

A: A shutterbug.

Q: What snake wears a crown on its head?

A: A king snake.

Q: What kind of bug does a cowboy ride?

A: A horsefly.

Q: What kind of coffeepots do cats use?

A: Purr-colators.

Q: What kind of insects do campers like?

A: Fireflies.

Q: Why did the fat cat get even fatter?

A: He ate at every oppor-tuna-ty.

This book is available in two editions:
Library binding by Carolrhoda Books, Inc.,
  a division of Lerner Publishing Group
Soft cover by First Avenue Editions,
  an imprint of Lerner Publishing Group
241 First Avenue North
Minneapolis, MN 55401

Website address: www.lernerbooks.com

Library of Congress Cataloging-in-Publication Data

Burns, Diane L.
    Backyard beasties : jokes that snake you smile / by Diane L. Burns and
Peter and Connie Roop ; pictures by Brian Gable.
        p.   cm. — (Make me laugh)
    Summary: A collection of jokes about backyard animals.
    ISBN: 1–57505–646–1 (lib. bdg. : alk. paper)
    ISBN: 1–57505–704–2 (pbk. : alk. paper)
    1. Animals—Juvenile humor. [1. Animals—Humor. 2. Jokes. 3. Riddles.
4. Puns and punning.] I. Roop, Peter. II. Roop, Connie. III. Gable, Brian, 1949–
ill. IV. Title. V. Series.
PN6231.A5 B87 2004
398.6—dc21   2002151105

Manufactured in the United States of America
1 2 3 4 5 6 – JR – 09 08 07 06 05 04